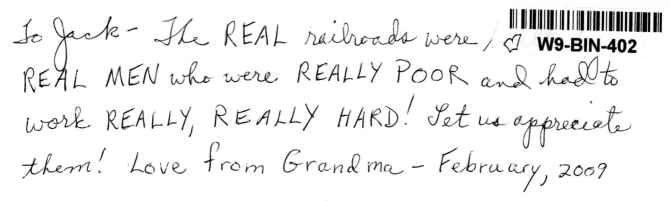

To Jack — The REAL railroads were /♡ **W9-BIN-402**
REAL MEN who were REALLY POOR and had to
work REALLY, REALLY HARD! Let us appreciate
them! Love from Grandma — February, 2009

Author:

Ian Graham studied applied physics at the City University, London. He then took a postgraduate degree in journalism, specializing in science and technology. Since becoming a freelance author and journalist, he has written more than one hundred children's non-fiction books.

Artist:

David Antram was born in Brighton in 1958. He studied at Eastbourne College of Art and then worked in advertising for 15 years before becoming a full-time artist. He has illustrated many children's non-fiction books.

Series Creator:

David Salariya was born in Dundee, Scotland. He has illustrated a wide range of books and has created and designed many new series for publishers both in the U.K. and overseas. In 1989, he established The Salariya Book Company. He lives in Brighton with his wife, illustrator Shirley Willis, and their son Jonathan.

Editor:

Karen Barker Smith

Assistant Editor:

Stephanie Cole

© The Salariya Book Company Ltd MMI

Created, designed, and produced by
The Salariya Book Company Ltd
25 Marlborough Place, Brighton BN1 1UB

Visit the Salariya Book Company at:
www.salariya.com

ISBN 13: 978-0-531-14603-3 (lib. bdg.)   978-0-531-16208-8 (pbk.)
ISBN-10: 0-531-14603-0 (lib. bdg.)   0-531-16208-7 (pbk.)

Published in the United States by Franklin Watts, a Division of Scholastic Inc.
90 Sherman Turnpike, Danbury, CT 06816

A CIP catalog record for this title is available from the Library of Congress.

Printed and bound in China.

Printed on paper from sustainable forests.

Reprinted in 2008.

You Wouldn't Want to Work on the Railroad!

Written by
Ian Graham

Illustrated by
David Antram

Created and designed by
David Salariya

A Track You'd Rather Not Go Down

W
FRANKLIN WATTS
A Division of Scholastic Inc.
NEW YORK • TORONTO • LONDON • AUCKLAND • SYDNEY
MEXICO CITY • NEW DELHI • HONG KONG
DANBURY, CONNECTICUT

Contents

Introduction

You are a farmworker in County Galway, Ireland, in the mid-19th century. This is a bad time to work on the land in Ireland. Everyone is so poor that most people can afford to eat only potatoes, but the potato crop has failed every year from 1845 to 1849. It's a time that will become known as the Great Potato Famine. More than a million people die of starvation and disease, and about 1.5 million more leave Ireland for North America in search of a better life. You stay for a while, but times are still so hard by 1860 that you finally decide to go, too.

You leave Ireland with little more than the clothes on your back and sail to North America to start a new life. You land in New York City and look for work right away. So many other people are competing for jobs that you hitch a ride on a freight train and head inland. You move from farm to farm, working for a few days at each one, making just enough money to eat.

This isn't the easy life you hoped for. You look for something different to do and decide to try construction work. It's hard work, but there is plenty of it. You soon learn that the one thing you wouldn't want to be is a construction worker on the transcontinental railroad!

Get to Work!

You decide to join a growing army of railroad workers in Nevada. Thousands of Irishmen already working in the United States flock to the country's biggest construction project: building the transcontinental railroad. There still aren't enough workers, however. People are needed so urgently that thousands more are brought across the Pacific Ocean from China. The railroad company pays for the voyage — $40 by steamship, $35 by sailboat — but the workers have to pay it back out of their wages. The crossing takes up to forty days by steamship and longer by sailboat. Soon the world's biggest work force is ready for action.

Well, off to work we go!

Chinese laborer

The Laborers:

You don't have special work clothes, just your normal everyday clothes. Chinese workers wear blue blouses, baggy trousers, and "basket" hats. Some wear their pigtails down, while others coil them under their hat. The work is hard manual labor, and you have to provide your own tools — picks, shovels, axes, and hammers.

Handy Hint

Remember to wear a wide-brimmed hat to keep the sun off your head and neck. If you don't, you'll collapse from sunstroke!

Irish laborers

Puff!

YOU ARE PAID $35 a month. Chinese laborers earn a little less, at $30 a month. For that — about a dollar a day — you have to work from sunrise to sunset, no matter how many hours that might be.

Where Do We Lay the Tracks?

The Surveying Party:

THE SURVEYOR looks through a telescope at a pole in the distance.

Surveyor

THE RODMAN holds the pole, which is marked so that the surveyor can see the slope of the land.

THE FLAGMAN sends messages between the surveyor and the rodman by waving a flag.

THE AXEMAN cuts down any trees that get in the way.

Rodman   *Flagman*

THE CHAINMAN measures the distance from the surveyor to the rodman.

Chainman

Axeman

Hunter   *Herder*

HERDERS drive cattle along with the survey gang to provide meat.

HUNTERS go along instead of herders if there are wild animals to eat.

Surveyors go ahead of the construction workers to find the best route for the track. It must not be too steep or cross too many rivers, valleys, or mountains. Surveyors work in gangs of about twenty men traveling on horseback. When they find the best route, they tap wooden stakes into the ground to guide the construction workers. You join a survey gang as an axeman. Your job is to cut down any trees that block the surveyors' line of sight.

The railroad will stretch across two-thirds of the United States, spanning a distance of 1,725 miles (2,776 km). It will go from Omaha, Nebraska, to Sacramento, California.

The railroad

Oregon

Idaho

California

Nevada

Utah

SACRAMENTO

San Francisco

9

Dig, Dig, Dig!

Now it's time to start work with the construction team. You are put to work as a grader, which means you must prepare the grade (ground) for the tracklayers who follow you. You have to transform the bumpy, rocky ground into a firm, even base for the track — no easy task! Power tools are scarce, so you have to move the soil and rock by hand, using picks, shovels, and wheelbarrows. It's back-breaking work, and you're outside in all types of weather. You have to work fast because the tracklayers aren't far behind, and you can't let them catch up with you.

DELIVERING SUPPLIES. The railway line doesn't reach as far as the graders. This means that all your supplies of food and water, and any new workers, are carried from the end of the railroad line to the construction site by horse-drawn wagons.

IF THE TRACK HAS TO CLIMB upward to higher ground, the graders have to build an earth embankment to support it. It can rise no more than 116 feet (35 m) in every mile.

Handy Hint
Look after your tools. If you break them, you will have to buy new ones.

SNAP

I think I put my back out.

Puff!

Tracklaying

After working as a grader for a while, you get to learn what the tracklayers do by watching them at work. Soon you are given work in one of the tracklaying gangs. Yours is the worst job of all — lifting rails off the railcars and lowering them onto the ties. Each rail is 30 feet (9 m) long and weighs a knee-buckling 560 pounds (255 kg). It takes 4 men just to lift one. According to the railroad's gauge, the rails have to be laid exactly 4 feet 8 inches (142 cm) apart. After hours of this back-breaking work, the setting sun is a welcome sight. Finally, you can stop working!

Tremble

Step by Step:

TIES. Wooden beams called ties are laid on the ground, following the line of stakes put in by the surveyors.

Clatter!

RAILS. Rails delivered by train are unloaded quickly so that the supply train can back up to let the next one through.

RAILCARS. The materials are loaded onto small railcars. Horses pull them up to the workers at the end of the line.

That's it...just a bit further to the left.

Handy Hint

Keep a lookout for the foremen. They gallop up and down the line of workers on horseback, checking that everyone is working hard.

FISH PLATES. The rails are laid on the ties, and the ends are bolted together with metal plates called fish plates.

SPIKES. Workers fix the rails to the ties by hammering iron spikes through holes in the rails.

LEVELING. Finally, a gang props up ties that are too low and shovels dirt underneath them to level the track.

13

Life on the Line

What's for Dinner?

IRISH DIET.
The Irish laborers eat a simple diet of boiled beef, potatoes, beans, bread, butter, and black coffee.

CHINESE DIET.
The Chinese eat a more varied diet including fish, fruit, rice, cabbage, pork, oysters, and bamboo shoots.

Living conditions are harsh and basic. The company provides bunk cars for the men to sleep in, but when the weather is hot and dry, you sleep in the cooler air under canvas beside the track. You share a small tent with five other workers. It's hard to stay healthy. Disease spreads so easily among the workers that the railroad companies won't hire anyone who is sick. Chinese workers are checked for the most serious illnesses, such as smallpox, before they leave China.

WHEN IT'S TIME TO EAT, you get in line at the food wagon for a meal of meat and vegetables. It's simple food, but it's hot and filling.

Going Underground

I hope he has good aim!

Your next job is with a gang of workers who are digging tunnels. Soft soil and stony rubble can be dug out easily enough with spades, picks, and shovels. Rock, however, has to be broken up by blasting it with explosives. You hold a long metal pole against the rock while another man swings a sledgehammer at it to make a hole for the explosive charge. In some places, blasting goes on for 24 hours a day, so you can't get away from the noise — even when you're trying to sleep!

Blasting

POWDER. Once the holes are drilled, they are packed with black powder rammed in with straw or sand on top.

FUSE. Fuses in the holes are lit. You run for cover as the flames burn toward the explosives.

BOOM!

Handy Hint

If you want to keep your head, don't stand in line with the blasting holes when the charges go off!

Nitroglycerin

Nitroglycerin is a liquid explosive. It is eight times more powerful than black powder, but the workers hate it. Many of the tunnelers refuse to work with it because it's so dangerous. It can explode if it's dropped!

Look what I found...

CLEARING OUT. Before the dust settles, you're back in the tunnel clearing rubble.

Mind Your Step!

Finally, you get to do a job that you enjoy: working as a bridge-builder. Bridge-building teams work at least 20 miles (30 km) ahead of the graders, so that the bridges are finished before the tracklayers reach them. Some bridges are more than 125 feet (35 m) high and 700 feet (210 m) long.

Thousands of feet of timber are needed to build the trestle framework that will support the weight of the track and trains. Where possible, timber is cut from forests close to the line. Some timber is delivered already cut to size, but most of the wood is cut at the bridge by men using double-handed saws.

Building a Bridge

Swing!

Bridge-building begins with making a firm base of rock. Tree trunks called piles are driven into the soft ground, and the bridge is built on top of them.

PILING. A steam pile driver hammers 30-foot (9-m) tree trunks into the ground.

TIMBER. Axemen chop down trees to provide the timber needed to build the bridge.

GRANITE. Blocks of granite hauled by wagon are laid to form a base for the bridge.

PRE-DRILLING. The bridge timbers are cut to size and pre-drilled on the ground.

BUILDING. The bridge timbers are hoisted into place and fixed together with bolts.

19

Brrr! Working in the Snow

Walking on Snow:

WALKING ON DEEP SNOW is tiring because you keep sinking into it.

One of your worst experiences on the railroad is working in Nebraska in the depths of winter. You have to build snowsheds to stop snow drifts from burying the track. The ground is so hard that it can't be dug, and every inch has to be blasted out. You live in a shack underground and walk to work through tunnels in the snow. You don't see the sky for months. Some of the tunnels are 200 feet (60 m) long and wide enough to let two horse-drawn sleds pass each other.

YOU TRY SKIS called Norwegian snowshoes, but they don't help.

TRADITIONAL SNOWSHOES are best. They are made of wood and have leather lacing.

Oh no! The train's here early!

20

Remember to plug all the holes in your shack, or you'll have to shovel out lots of snow to get into it again.

IT'S SO COLD inside your shack (5 degrees below zero) that hot coffee turns into thick slush in minutes, and butter freezes solid.

A SNOW PLOW keeps the track clear, but it can't move the deepest snowdrifts, which have to be dug out by hand.

The Railroad Invasion

Working on the railroad gets more dangerous as the track reaches the Midwestern plains. These lands have been occupied by American Indian tribes for centuries. Most tribes see the railroad workers as invaders, so they attack them.

Survey parties and axemen cutting wood face the greatest danger because they work in small gangs away from the main construction teams. Raiding parties of Sioux and Cheyenne warriors are feared the most. Their attacks are such a serious problem that the railroad workers have to be protected by armed military escorts.

Drop everything! The Indians are here!

Whistle

SOLDIERS take their position on high ground overlooking the workers and watch for any sign of attack.

Handy Hint

When you're on your own, don't take pot shots at wild animals — you might attract attention from the local tribes!

Crack!

Gallop! Gallop!

AMERICAN INDIANS make things difficult for the railroad companies by placing logs and rocks on the line to derail supply trains.

WHEN WARRIORS attack your work team, you send smoke signals to summon help from soldiers waiting nearby in a troop train.

Let's Build a Town

The railroad companies build towns and stations at intervals along the track. Some are just temporary bases for stock-piling materials and housing workers. Others are permanent towns. At one, you help to put up some buildings. They are delivered by train in flat sections, which you have to nail together. It's hard work, but a welcome break from building the railroad. Merchants and traders build shops beside the stations to help the railroad workers spend their money. As more people arrive, houses, hotels, and banks are built to serve their needs.

SOME NEW RAILROAD TOWNS thrive and grow prosperous. Many temporary towns quickly die and become deserted "ghost towns" when the railroad and its workers move on.

24

Chuff Chuff Chuff

Thud!

Steer clear of the saloons and casinos, or you'll lose all your hard-earned money. Once your money's gone, you'll be booted out!

WATER TOWERS are a familiar sight along the track. They let locomotives fill their water tanks between stations.

LOCOMOTIVES loaded with supplies for the new towns can be unloaded and then sent back to where they came from by using a section of track laid on a huge turntable.

The Golden Spike

The big day finally arrives: the Union Pacific track, laid westward from Omaha, Nebraska, meets the Central Pacific track, laid eastward from Sacramento, California. The tracks meet at Promontory Summit, Utah. The Union Pacific locomotive *No. 119* noses up to the Central Pacific's *Jupiter*. As soon as the railroad company bosses and politicians arrive, the ceremony begins. You climb onto one of the locomotives to get a good view.

A railroad tie made of polished laurel wood is brought out and put under the rails. Leland Stanford of Central Pacific and Thomas Durant of Union Pacific tap two golden spikes into the tie with silver hammers. The world's first transcontinental railway is complete at last!

Handy Hint

Hang around the important men in suits — the railroad managers and government officials — and you might get a drink of their champagne!

PHOTOGRAPHERS take pictures that will soon appear in newspapers around the world.

THE GOLD SPIKES and laurel tie are quickly replaced. People take so many pieces off the new tie and rails that four rails and six ties have to be replaced as well!

Hooray!

TELEGRAPH OPERATORS send the message "Done" all over the nation. Within a few minutes, bells ring out in the cities, and millions of people know the line is finished.

What Good Is the Railroad Anyway?

When you are an old man, sitting in your rocking chair on the porch of your home in Sacramento, you show your grandchildren a faded photograph cut from a newspaper. It's a picture of the golden spike ceremony that completed the transcontinental railroad. You tell them about your part in building the railroad and how it changed American history. It opened up huge areas of land to settlers. Telegraph wires beside the track let people send messages from coast to coast. However, the railroad was a disaster for American Indians. Settlers took their land from them, and the railroad brought hunters who killed millions of the buffalo that Indian tribes depended on for food and clothing.

The Good:

TRANSPORT. Trains carry people and supplies into the hundreds of new towns that spring up along the railroad line.

SETTLERS. Farms, cattle ranches, and homesteads cluster around the new towns as settlers claim more and more land.

TELEGRAPH. Railroad companies use telegraph wires to send messages to stations about delays and accidents.

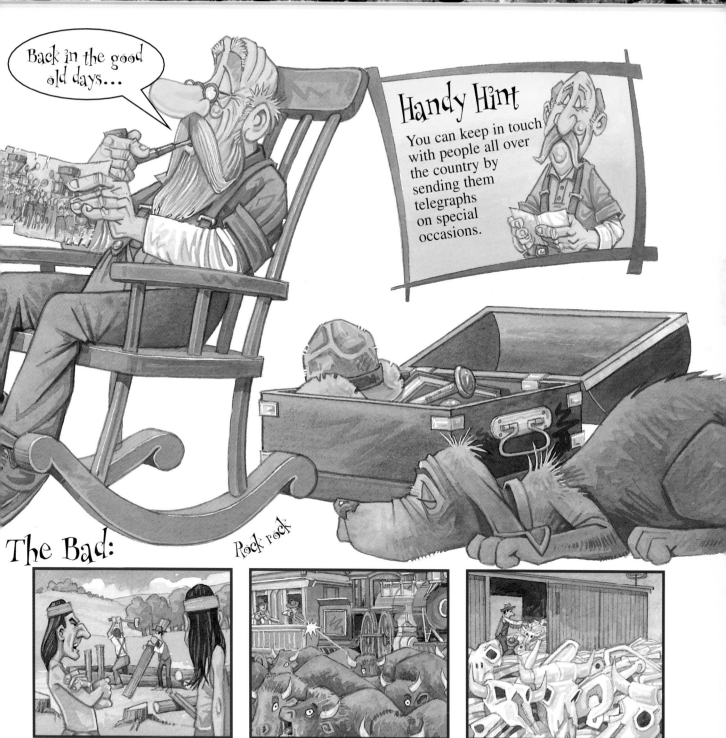

Handy Hint

You can keep in touch with people all over the country by sending them telegraphs on special occasions.

The Bad:

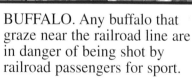

RESISTANCE. American Indian tribes, angered by the construction of the railroad, fight it all the way.

BUFFALO. Any buffalo that graze near the railroad line are in danger of being shot by railroad passengers for sport.

BONES. Tons of buffalo bones are loaded onto railroad wagons to be shipped out and made into plant fertilizer.

Glossary

Axeman A workman who cuts down trees or trims timber with an axe.

Bunk car A railroad car with beds for workers to sleep in.

Central Pacific The railroad company that built part of the transcontinental railroad from Sacramento, California, to Promontory Summit, Utah.

Chainman A worker who measures the distance from the surveyor to the rodman.

Fish plate A metal plate used to link the ends of two rails.

Flagman A worker who signals from a surveyor to a rodman by waving a flag.

Freight train A train that carries food and other supplies.

Fuse A cord used to set off an explosive charge. One end is pushed into the charge, and the other end is lit. The flame travels along the cord to the charge, which explodes.

Gauge The distance between the rails. The transcontinental railroad had a gauge of 4 feet 8 inches.

Grader A railroad worker who prepares the ground before railroad track is laid on it.

Herder A person who looks after the herds of cattle that are used as food by the railroad workers.

Leveler A railroad worker who follows the tracklayers and makes sure the track is level.

Locomotive An engine on wheels, used to pull railcars.

Merchant A trader.

Nitroglycerin A black oily liquid and powerful explosive used in railroad construction.

Pile A wooden log driven into soft ground to form a firm footing for a bridge.

Pile driver A steam-powered machine used to drive piles into the ground by dropping a heavy weight on them.

Powder keg A small barrel of blasting powder.

Railcar A passenger carriage, or an open railway truck for transporting construction materials.

Rodman A worker who holds a measuring rod for a surveyor.

Snow plow A tool shaped like a farm plow, used for clearing snow.

Surveyor Someone who goes ahead of railroad workers to map the ground and decides where the tracks will be laid.

Telegraph A system for sending messages over long distances as electric currents traveling along wires.

Tie A wooden beam laid on the ground to support the rails.

Transcontinental Crossing a whole continent.

Trestle A wooden frame that forms part of a railway bridge, supporting the weight of the track.

Turntable A circular wooden platform used to turn a locomotive around.

Union Pacific The railroad company that built part of the transcontinental railroad from Omaha, Nebraska, to Promontory Summit, Utah.

Index